THE VOICE OF FOOTBALL
SHOOT
D0262313
Capital One Cup
/TheVoiceOfFootball
WWW.SHOOT.CO.UK
@_shootfootball
ANNUAL/DEPUTY EDITOR: James Beavis ASSISTANT EDITOR: Dan Church

Surely, it couldn't get any better? Oh, it could! The Etihad Stadium was the next venue for Rashford - the home of United's arch-rivals, Manchester City.

A month after introducing himself to the game; the teenager became the youngest ever goalscorer in a Manchester derby in the Premier League era, after netting the only goal of the game as the city was painted red.

Rashford's phenomenal form for the remainder of the 2015/16 season saw then England manager Roy Hodgson include the Red Devils starlet in his preliminary 26-man squad for the European Championships in France, providing United's local lad with an opportunity to make his name heard all over the world.

And it didn't take him long! Just 135 seconds into his Three Lions bow, Rashford opened the scoring against Australia in a friendly to become the youngest English player to score on his senior international debut.

Four days later; the forward's strike at the Stadium of Light helped him weave his way into Hodgson's final 23-man squad for EURO 2016 - joining the likes of Wayne Rooney, Harry Kane, Jamie Vardy and Daniel Sturridge, in a bid to fire England to glory.

It was in Lens on June 16, 2016, that Rashford worked his way into the record books once again, replacing Adam Lallana in the 73rd minute of England's 2-1 victory over Wales to become the youngest player to feature at the finals in France.

He also surpassed another one of captain Rooney's honours, snatching the achievement of becoming his country's youngest ever player to star at the European Championships - by just four days!

However; it could have been a very different story for United's teen sensation, as a potential loan move away from Old Trafford was on the cards - just a week before he made his memorable debut inside the Theatre of Dreams.

Crewe Alexandra previously approached United to sign Rashford on loan, only for the club to tell the Football League outfit he was needed for their Under-21 side, before the then 18-year-old's instant success.

Having started his footballing path at the age of five with Fletcher Moss Rangers - the Red Devils' goldmine of a community club - Rashford has already put pen to paper on a new deal to keep him at Manchester United until 2020.

Following in the footsteps of the likes of Wes Brown, Danny Welbeck and Cameron Borthwick-Jackson in graduating from Didsbury's most successful junior side; Rashford is tipped to become a prolific centre-forward for both club and country.

DID YOU KNOW?

Rashford scored four goals from his first five shots for Manchester United.

WHAT HE SAYS:

"When I first went into the [England] changing room and saw all of the players' names on the back of their shirts, it didn't seem real."

FACT FILE

MARCUS RASHFORD

Position: Striker
Height: 1.80m
Birth Date: October 31, 1997
Birth Place: Manchester; England
Clubs: Manchester United
International: England

PREMIER LEAGUE 2015/16 STATS:

Games: 11
Goals: 5
Assists: 2
Key passes: 4
Shots: 9
Shot accuracy: 89%
Pass accuracy: 77%
Take ons: 9
Yellow cards: 0
Red cards: 0

4 HOW IMPORTANT IS IT TO BE ABLE TO SHOOT WITH YOUR WEAKER FOOT?

"That is a big part of my finishing. I think if you can score with both feet, then it just adds so many more goals to your game. You can't always control where the ball is on the pitch and where the ball is going to fall, so you have just got to be ready if it does fall to you on your weaker foot and put it in the back of the net."

5 HOW HARD IS IT TO LEAD THE LINE?

"It is definitely something you have to practice. I have done a lot of work with the manager on how he wanted me to do that. It is difficult because you always normally have two centre-backs behind you, as well as a sitting midfielder, so you obviously need to be strong, hold the ball up and make sure you bring others into play. You try and keep a high line for the creative players; so the number tens get on the ball, then you can make your run and hopefully you'll get it back."

6 HOW DO YOU LOSE YOUR MARKER AND FIND SPACE IN THE BOX?

"I think it is about looking where the defender is and just drifting into spaces where they probably don't think the ball is going to go. I think a lot of it is instinct. When I am in the box, I just sort of feel a position where the ball might fall and try and get in there and hope the defender doesn't read it."

7 HOW DO YOU WIN HEADERS IN THE PENALTY AREA?

"Early jump, for me. I think if you can get that run and jump on the defender, then it will be very difficult for him to stop you. It always seems like they are trying to head it out, whereas if you are running and heading it forward, not many people are going to stop you. It is about timing."

8 YOU ARE ONE-ON-ONE WITH THE GOALKEEPER, WHAT DO YOU DO?

"It all depends on how much time I have. If I have lots of time, I will probably try and take the goalkeeper on. If there is a defender chasing me, then I normally just try and open up my body, depending whether I am on my right or left foot. I will then try and open my body towards the far corner."

9 WHAT ADVICE WOULD YOU GIVE ON PENALTIES?

"To be confident. For me personally; I practise a lot down the left, down the middle and to the right. You need to try and prepare for any situation, so get a lot of practice. I have a foot pattern that I do before every penalty, so make sure you get used to that and just be confident."

10 WHAT ARE YOUR TOP 3 TIPS FOR KIDS ASPIRING TO BECOME A FOOTBALLER?

"To work hard, of course. You have got to put in the practice and make sure you are working harder than anybody else. To believe in yourself; because if you don't believe in yourself, then not many other people will believe in you. And to be confident. Believe you are the best and go out there and make it happen."

MEN'S 4X100M RELAY

Theo Walcott, Kyle Walker, Jamie Vardy and Hector Bellerin

This fearsome foursome could give Usain Bolt and his Jamaican teammates a run for their money, with Arsenal right-back Bellerin clocking an astonishing 4.41 seconds over 40 metres!

It proved to be a very busy summer for some of the world's best footballers at the Euros in France, but what if they were also eligible to compete in athletics? Which players and managers would feature in which events?

Shoot selects a cluster of footballing stars who could make the cut in their specialist sport.

WEIGHTLIFTING

Adebayo Akinfenwa

Everyone's FIFA favourite wouldn't look out of place among the world's strongest weightlifters, with the Wycombe Wanderers striker able to bench press a staggering 190kg - almost DOUBLE his body weight!

DIVING

Ashley Young

Unfortunately the Manchester United winger is regarded as one of the Premier League's worst 'divers', so it wouldn't be a surprise to see Young make a splash from a three-metre springboard alongside Great Britain's Tom Daley.

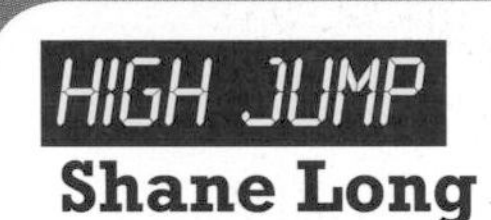

HIGH JUMP

Shane Long

Despite being 5ft 11in; the Southampton striker possesses one of the largest leaps in the Premier League, with the Irishman renowned for superbly heading home crosses into the back of the net.

GYMNASTICS
Pierre-Emerick Aubameyang

Having scored a sensational 39 goals in all competitions last season for Borussia Dortmund, fans have had plenty of chances to savour the prolific striker's perfectly executed front flip goal celebration – 10/10 from *Shoot*!

MARATHON
N'Golo Kante

Move over Mo Farah; France international Kante could pip you to the finish line over 26.2 miles given the midfielder's engine and relentless work rate all over the pitch. It's tiring just watching him!

WRESTLING
Diego Costa

The Chelsea hitman loves a good scuffle on the pitch, so he should have no problem taking on the likes of John Cena and Roman Reigns from WWE!

BASKETBALL
Cristiano Ronaldo

The Real Madrid forward is known for his great leap in the air, and even basketball's finest players would find it difficult to snatch the ball off the Portuguese slam-dunker!

SWIMMING
Louis van Gaal

The former Manchester United manager was keen to show off his backstroke technique in front of fourth official Mike Dean last season. Unfortunately for Van Gaal, Old Trafford's touchline isn't the best place to take a dip!

HANDBALL
David De Gea

The Manchester United shot-stopper would have been a welcome addition to Spain's national handball team given the Spaniard's outstanding reflexes and handling skills.

ARCHERY
Mesut Ozil

Accuracy is the Arsenal ace's middle name, and Ozil would surely be clinical from up to 90 metres out with a bow and arrow given the German's exquisite precision.

VIRGIL VAN DIJK

DID YOU KNOW?

Van Dijk signed a new six-year deal with Southampton in May 2016.

WHAT THEY SAY:

"I think he's been terrific and it's a real sign to everyone in the world that Southampton mean business."
James Ward-Prowse, Southampton teammate.

CLUB: SOUTHAMPTON
HEIGHT: 1.93m
DATE OF BIRTH: JULY 8, 1991
PLACE OF BIRTH: BREDA, NETHERLANDS
INTERNATIONAL: NETHERLANDS

COLOUR IN THE STARS AND RATE VAN DIJK

ENDERSDEFEND

JAN VERTONGHEN

DID YOU KNOW?

Vertonghen won the Dutch league twice as a player with Ajax.

WHAT THEY SAY:

"He is strong defensively and contributes offensively too."
Toby Alderweireld, Tottenham and Belgium teammate.

CLUB: TOTTENHAM
HEIGHT: 1.89m
DATE OF BIRTH: APRIL 24, 1987
PLACE OF BIRTH: SINT-NIKLAAS, BELGIUM
INTERNATIONAL: BELGIUM

COLOUR IN THE STARS AND RATE VERTONGHEN

How do you look after debutants or young players in the squad?

"As captain, my role is to make sure that they feel comfortable in the first-team squad. When I joined the England squad as a 17-year-old, Faye White was the captain and she was the first person to come up to me and check I was okay. That has always stuck in my memory. That was a massive moment."

DID YOU KNOW?
Houghton was named England captain in 2014.

What do you say in the pre-match huddles?

"I am lucky that I have already got a squad that are focused. I think a lot of my job is just to reiterate what the manager has said and remind them about the importance of starting well. It is all about the team and about what you can do to make sure that the team wins."

Are you in charge of the pre-match music in the dressing room?

"Certainly not! That is too much pressure for me. I think there are a few girls that fight over the music, whether that is Alex Scott, Lucy Bronze or Karen Bardsley. There is a mixture of music played, but Drake and Beyonce are quite popular."

What are your three key tips for kids aspiring to be a captain?

"Firstly, communication is a massive thing. It is important to listen to your teammates and staff. Two; don't try and be anybody apart from yourself. You have been picked as captain for a reason and that is because of the personal traits you have. And three; probably the most important one, is to enjoy it. Sometimes it's hard to enjoy it because there is so much responsibility and pressure. But when you win, it's the best feeling in the world."

STEPH HOUGHTON FACT FILE

Height: 1.72m
Date of Birth: April 23, 1988
Place of Birth: Durham, England
Clubs: Manchester City Ladies
International: England

KEY
A
B
C
D
E
F
G
H
I
J
K
L
M
N
O
P
Q
R
S
T
U
V
W
X
Y
Z

★GYM RECORDS★

AKINFENWA CAN BENCH PRESS 190kg (The same as a male adult lion or two Romelu Lukaku's)

Q How will you feel when another player takes your reign as FIFA's strongest player?

"I'm losing it when I retire! I am telling you that now. At 34, I feel stronger than I ever have. Unless I see the person and am like, "Yeah, he can push 190 kg. This guy is strong," then I would happily relinquish my crown. But until I see that, me and head office at FIFA are going to have a problem!"

Did you know?

Akinfenwa supports Liverpool and scored against his favourite team in the FA Cup back in January 2015.

Q What will you do when you retire from football?

"I took my kids to the wrestling when they came over to the UK, and I looked at it and thought I could do that. But I am big on the whole 'Beast Mode On' stuff in the sense of doing mentoring. We are also starting up a BMO football academy, so watch this space!"

Q How does your super strength help you on the pitch?

"My superpower is my strength. When it comes to ball retention and bringing others into play, that is my strength. But with my strength, it means that I am not the quickest, so I have got to try and balance it up. But it helps me immensely in the sense that not many people can get the ball off me, I am very good at bringing others into play."

Q How have you dealt with the fame given your popular FIFA gaming stature?

"It is just mad. I will be going to like Westfield and my kids are like, "Daddy, why do people want to take your picture?" I am blessed in the sense that I play lower league football, but my profile is that of a Premier League footballer. It is a nice feeling and it does show that hard work does pay off in that sense. It just shows that if you believe it, you can achieve it."

Q What do you do in the gym and how often do you train?

"I try and gym four times a week, which consists of 90-100 minute sessions. At the club; we train three or four times a week, so I try and do double sessions and go to the gym in the evening. Then the eating, I enjoy chicken! Nando's is up there. Eat chicken and train – those are the two things if you want to get big!"

Q What was your inspiration to become so strong?

"It came from my brothers. If you look at the three of us together, we look like a wrestling trio. We are some big boys. So when growing up, I learnt early that if I wasn't big enough, I wasn't going to eat at night! It was survival of the fittest."

Q If you weren't a footballer, what would you have been?

"I would have been doing something where I could work with kids. I have always been charismatic, so maybe a teacher or a dance choreographer. You didn't know back in the day that I could dance! I tell you that I could dance. I'll show you some moves later!"

LIONEL MESSI

DID YOU KNOW?

Messi scored his 500th career goal in April 2016.

WHAT THEY SAY:

"I knew from the first time I saw him play that he was from a different planet. I believe that he's the best player in the history of football."
Gerard Pique, Barcelona teammate.

CLUB: BARCELONA

HEIGHT: 1.70m

DATE OF BIRTH: JUNE 24, 1987

PLACE OF BIRTH: ROSARIO, ARGENTINA

INTERNATIONAL: ARGENTINA

COLOUR IN THE STARS AND RATE MESSI

FORWARDSFORWARDS

WAYNE ROONEY

DID YOU KNOW?

Rooney was approached by the Republic of Ireland at just 16 years of age, but he rejected them so he could play for England.

WHAT THEY SAY:

"For me, he is the great English player of the generation."
Lionel Messi, Barcelona forward.

CLUB: MANCHESTER UNITED

HEIGHT: 1.76m

DATE OF BIRTH: OCTOBER 24, 1985

PLACE OF BIRTH: LIVERPOOL

INTERNATIONAL: ENGLAND

COLOUR IN THE STARS AND RATE ROONEY

ELLEN WHITE

CLUB: NOTTS COUNTY LADIES

HEIGHT: 1.70m

DATE OF BIRTH: MAY 9, 1989

PLACE OF BIRTH: AYLESBURY, ENGLAND

INTERNATIONAL: ENGLAND

DID YOU KNOW?

White scored on her international debut in England's 3-0 win over Austria in March 2010.

WHAT THEY SAY:

"I am really pleased with how I look [on FIFA] and they got my quiff perfect! My husband is looking forward to playing the game and being able to control me!"

PER LEAGUESUP

TONI DUGGAN

CLUB: MANCHESTER CITY LADIES

HEIGHT: 1.68m

DATE OF BIRTH: JULY 25, 1991

PLACE OF BIRTH: LIVERPOOL, ENGLAND

INTERNATIONAL: ENGLAND

DID YOU KNOW?

Duggan was working full-time for a five-a-side football centre when she started her career at Everton.

WHAT THEY SAY:

"If I want to be at the top, Man City is the best club for me. The women are treated exactly the same as the men, they've built a mini stadium just for the women's team!"

"MAYBE IF I JUST PULL THIS OVER MY EYES!"
THIS IRISH FAN COULDN'T BEAR TO WATCH HIS TEAM ANY MORE!
"WHAT DO YOU MEAN THESE TRACKSUIT BOTTOMS AREN'T FASHIONABLE ANY MORE?!"
ALMOST THERE!
GRANQVIST GETS SOME HELP FROM SHANE LONG AS HE ATTEMPTS HIS FIRST-EVER HANDSTAND!
LOUIS VAN FALL
LVG ISN'T HAPPY WHEN HE FAILS TO WIN A FREE-KICK AND IS ACCUSED OF DIVING!
GREAT BULL CONTROL!
HEREFORD SHOW THEY HAVE THE SKILL ON AND OFF THE PITCH AT WEMBLEY!
"DO YOU THINK ANYONE HAS NOTICED, SERGIO?"
RAMOS AND INIESTA AREN'T FOOLING ANYONE WITH THEIR DISGUISES!